EDGE BOOKS

BMX EXTREME

BMX HISTORY

by Brian D. Fiske

Consultant:
Keith Mulligan
Editor/Photographer
TransWorld BMX Magazine

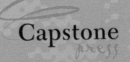

Capstone
press

Mankato, Minnesota

Edge Books are published by Capstone Press
151 Good Counsel Drive, P.O. Box 669, Mankato, Minnesota 56002
www.capstonepress.com

Library of Congress Cataloging-in-Publication Data
Fiske, Brian D.
    BMX history / by Brian D. Fiske.
    p. cm.—(Edge books. BMX extreme)
    Summary: Describes the history of bicycle motocross, including the major events
and athletes in the sport.
    Includes bibliographical references and index.
    ISBN 0-7368-2435-9 (hardcover)
    1. Bicycle motocross—History—Juvenile literature. [1. Bicycle motocross.
2. Bicycle racing.] I. Title. II. Series.
GV1049.3.F59 2004
796.6'2—dc22   2003013714

Editorial Credits

Angela Kaelberer, editor; Enoch Peterson, series designer; Jason Knudson,
    book designer; Jo Miller, photo researcher

Photo Credits

Bruce Mulligan, 20
Getty Images/Elsa, 28; Mark Mainz, 25; Stanley Chou, 8
Keith Mulligan/TransWorld BMX, cover, 5, 7, 12, 14, 24, 26, 27
Lillethorup Productions Inc./Frank Sklenicka, 19; Steve Goodnight, 17
Scot "OM" Breithaupt, 11
SportsChrome-USA/Scott Clarke, 23

1 2 3 4 5 6 09 08 07 06 05 04

Table of Contents

CHAPTER 1

Bicycle Motocross

On May 7, 2000, BMX freestyle riders and fans filled the Utopia International Park in Raleigh, North Carolina. The riders and fans were there for the park finals of the Crazy Freakin' Bikers (CFB) contest.

Dave Mirra had a surprise planned. He wanted to do a double backflip. No rider had ever completed this trick in competition.

Learn about:

- Double backflip
- BMX bikes
- Events

4

Dave Mirra hoped to land a double backflip in competition.

Mirra dropped in on the ramp and pedaled hard to build his speed. He hit the box jump and sailed high into the air. Mirra flipped his bike backward in the air not just once, but twice. The riders and fans cheered. Mirra had just landed the first BMX double backflip ever in competition.

Three months later, Mirra did another double backflip at the X Games in San Francisco, California. Mirra's trick helped him win a gold medal. It was the ninth X Games gold medal of his career.

Mirra's double backflip won him a gold medal at the 2000 X Games.

Freestyle BMX riders do tricks at the X Games and other competitions.

BMX

Bicycle motocross (BMX) racing began in 1969 in southern California. There, people started racing bikes on motocross tracks. The races quickly grew from 10 or 20 riders to several hundred. Within 10 years, BMX had millions of riders and fans all over the world.

BMX bikes are different from other bikes. They are smaller and have wider tires to better grip the ground. They are made of strong materials such as chromoly steel alloy. The bikes' high handlebars tilt slightly toward the rider.

BMX riders compete in several types of events. Freestyle riders do tricks at the X Games, the Gravity Games, and other judged events. Other riders race on dirt tracks, some with paved turns. Still others race on downhill tracks.

The Early Days

In 1969, a group of kids in Santa Monica, California, wanted to race bikes on dirt trails at a local park. Park worker Ron Mackler helped the kids organize the first registered BMX race.

First BMX Bike

The Schwinn Stingray was the most popular bike used in early BMX races. The Stingray was not built for BMX, but it had strong 20-inch (51-centimeter) wheels. Today's BMX bikes still use wheels of this size.

Learn about:

- Schwinn Stingray
- Modifications
- *On Any Sunday*

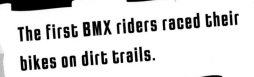

The first BMX riders raced their
bikes on dirt trails.

Rider Changes

Over time, BMX racers changed the Stingrays to meet their needs. One of the first changes was made to the bikes' forks. The fork supports the front wheel and works with the handlebars

Early BMX bikes had shock absorbers on both the frame and the fork.

to turn the front wheel. The Stingray's fork was not strong. Riders often bent their forks during jumps or crashes.

Racers designed and built larger and stronger forks for their bikes. Other new BMX parts were developed the same way. Riders noticed the weak spots on their bikes and invented new parts to solve the problems.

BMX in the Movies

In 1971, a movie about motorcycle riding and racing was released. The movie was called *On Any Sunday.*

The beginning of the movie shows a BMX race. That short scene caught the attention of motorcycle racers around the country. Many riders had children who liked racing but were too young to ride motorcycles. Adult motorcycle racers started organizing BMX races, and the sport's popularity grew.

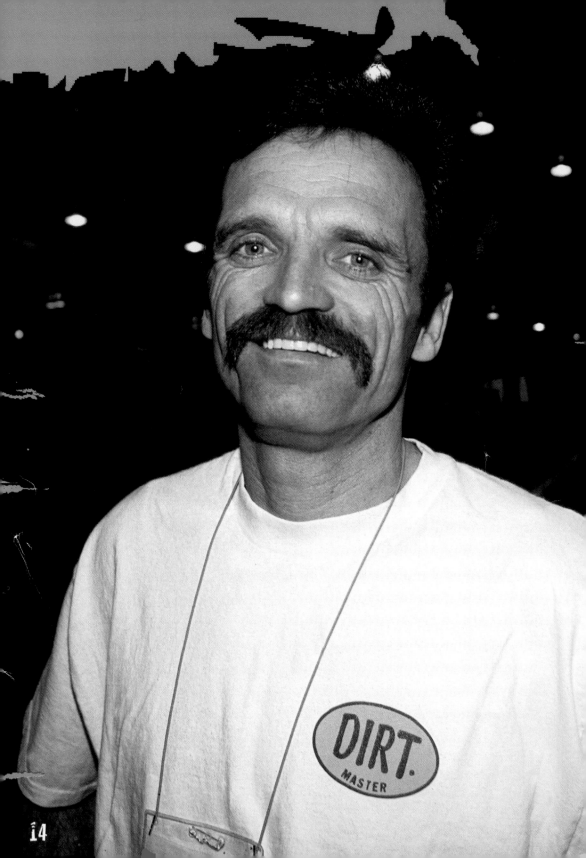

Scot Breithaupt

Many people consider Scot Breithaupt the founder of BMX. In 1970, 14-year-old Breithaupt asked 30 young riders to compete in a race in his hometown of Long Beach, California. Each rider paid 25 cents to compete. The next weekend, 150 riders came to race.

Breithaupt continued to compete and put on races until the late 1980s. He also started his own bicycle company, SE Racing. The American Bicycle Association, the International BMX Federation, and the National Bicycle League have all named Breithaupt to their halls of fame.

CHAPTER 3

Growth of BMX

In 1974, a motorcycle frame company called Red Line Engineering became the first company to make a part just for BMX bikes. The part was a sturdy fork made of chromoly. The same year, the Webco Company made the first production BMX bike frame.

Soon, motorcycle companies began making bikes designed for BMX. Yamaha and Kawasaki were the first major companies to make BMX bikes. Graco also made an early BMX bike.

Learn about:

- Early BMX companies
- Organizations
- Early freestyle riders

Graco was one of the first companies to make a bike designed for BMX.

BMX Gets Organized

In 1973, BMX track owner Ernie Alexander founded the National Bicycle Association (NBA) in California. This group was the first nationwide BMX organization.

The next year, the NBA helped put on the first large BMX event. The Yamaha Gold Cup Series included several races in Los Angeles and San Diego, California. The championship race was held in the Los Angeles Coliseum. About 1,000 riders and 16,000 fans were at the race. *Sports Illustrated* magazine published a story on the event. Many people who read the story became interested in BMX.

NBL and ABA

In 1974, George Esser started the National Bicycle League (NBL) in Pompano Beach, Florida. Earlier, Esser had started the National Motorcycle League (NML). The NBL hosted its first race in January 1974 at the Miami-Hollywood Speedway Park in Florida. Soon, it held races in other states as well.

In 1977, the American Bicycle Association (ABA) formed. The NBL and the ABA still put on most BMX races in the United States.

The ABA put on many races after it formed in 1977.

The movie *Rad* was released in 1986. This movie about bike racers helped spread BMX's popularity.

BMX racing was most popular in the mid-1980s.

From Racing to Freestyle

BMX racing reached its top popularity in the mid-1980s. As racing became less popular, another kind of BMX riding was growing. Some riders started doing tricks and jumps on their bikes. Riders called the new sport freestyle.

In 1979, *BMX ACTION* magazine editor Bob Osborn wanted to form a freestyle team. Osborn's son, R. L., joined with Bob Haro to form the *BMX ACTION* Trick Team. Osborn and Haro put on freestyle shows all over the United States.

Growth of Freestyle

Freestyle became even more popular in the 1980s. Riders held competitions in skateboard parks to see who could do the best tricks.

In 1982, 18-year-old rider Bob Morales formed the Amateur Skate Park Association to promote freestyle riding. Later, this group became the American Freestyle Association. The AFA put on many freestyle competitions, but the biggest events were yet to come.

CHAPTER 4

BMX Today

In the early 1990s, BMX stunts caught the attention of people at the ESPN TV network. The network was organizing the first extreme sports competition, the Extreme Games. Today, this event is called the X Games.

In 1995, freestyle BMX riders competed in the first Extreme Games in Providence, Rhode Island. Many people watched Dave Mirra, Mat Hoffman, and other top riders compete at the event.

Since 2000, freestyle riders have competed in the Gravity Games. The NBC TV network hosts this extreme sports event.

Learn about:

- X Games
- Freestyle BMX
- Modern racing

Each year, freestyle riders show off their skills at the X Games.

Freestyle Events

Freestyle riders compete in four types of events. These events are dirt, flatland, park, and vert. Dirt riders perform stunts in the air over mounds of dirt built just for jumping. Flatland riders do tricks on paved, level surfaces such as parking lots.

Flatland riders do tricks on level surfaces.

Park riding is also called street riding. Park riders do tricks on courses that have box jumps, ramps of different sizes, and other obstacles.

Vert riders do tricks on large ramps called halfpipes. Most of these U-shaped ramps are between 10 and 13 feet (3 and 4 meters) high.

Downhill BMX racers compete in the X Games.

Today's Races

BMX races are still popular with many fans. The NBL and the ABA hold races in the United States and Canada. Each August, top racers compete in the NBL Grand Nationals. Racers call this race the "Grands." The ABA holds its Grand Nationals in November.

In 2001, people watching the X Games saw a new form of BMX racing. Downhill racers sped down dirt courses that were about 1,500 feet (460 meters) long. They sailed over jumps and other obstacles as long as 40 feet (12 meters). Downhill races are still part of the X Games and other competitions.

Each August, racers compete in the NBL Grands.

Freestyle riders combine skill with creativity.

Future of BMX

BMX's popularity is not a surprise. Young people created the sport, but almost any rider can enjoy it. Riders who want speed and group competition can test their skills in a race. Riders who like to show their creativity can try freestyle. With more riders trying BMX each year, it will remain a top extreme sport in the future.

Glossary

chromoly (kroh-MAWL-ee)—a mixture of metals used to make bike frames

frame (FRAYM)—the body of a bike

freestyle (FREE-stile)—a type of BMX riding that focuses on tricks and jumps

halfpipe (HAF-pipe)—a U-shaped ramp with high walls; freestyle riders use halfpipes to do tricks.

motocross (MOH-toh-kross)—a sport in which people race motorcycles on dirt courses

obstacle (OB-stuh-kuhl)—an object such as a ramp or box jump; park BMX riders do tricks on obstacles.

Read More

Deady, Kathleen W. *BMX Bikes*. Wild Rides! Mankato, Minn.: Capstone Press, 2002.

Dick, Scott. *BMX*. Radical Sports. Chicago: Heinemann Library, 2003.

Herran, Joe, and Ron Thomas. *BMX Riding*. Action Sports. Philadelphia: Chelsea House, 2003.

Useful Addresses

American Bicycle Association
P.O. Box 718
Chandler, AZ 85244

National Bicycle League
3958 Brown Park Drive, Suite D
Hilliard, OH 43026

TransWorld BMX
1421 Edinger Avenue, Suite D
Tustin, CA 92780

Internet Sites

FactHound offers a safe, fun way to find Internet sites related to this book. All of the sites on FactHound have been researched by our staff.

Here's how:

1. Visit *www.facthound.com*
2. Type in this special code **0736824359** for age-appropriate sites. Or enter a search word related to this book for a more general search.
3. Click on the **Fetch It** button.

FactHound will fetch the best sites for you!

Index